SPRING INTO EASTER

Edited by

Steph Park-Pirie

First published in Great Britain in 2004 by
TRIUMPH HOUSE
Remus House,
Coltsfoot Drive,
Peterborough, PE2 9JX
Telephone (01733) 898102

All Rights Reserved

Copyright Contributors 2004

SB ISBN 1 84431 073 6

Foreword

In today's modern world everyone's life is fast-moving and hectic, leaving little time to stop, open our minds and gather together our thoughts. However, there are times when we really do need to take time out to sort our feelings and emotions. Poetry can very often provide us much-needed release by allowing us to express and share our important thoughts with others.

Spring Into Easter is a special collection of these poems, featuring the work of over 120 new and established authors of today.

Together they combine their creative talents to present to you an inspiring and enjoyable read that you will want to return to time and time again.

Steph Park-Pirie
Editor

CONTENTS

A Springtime Morning	Robert Basham	1
Easter Changes	Walter Dalton	2
Easter In Scotland 2002	Audrey Marshall	3
Easter Morning, Ballyculter	John Potter	4
In Pamphill Wood (Dorset)	Sammy Michael Davis	6
Easter	Chris Thomas	7
Easter	Beryl Van Donk	8
An Unlucky Break	Alan Dudeney	9
Words From The Cross	Christina Miller	10
Multiplication	A Wilcox	11
April Day	David Mitchell	12
Easter	Alex O'Grady	13
Easter For Me (I)	Delroy Dwyer	14
Easter Is Here	Ashleigh Rice	16
Chocolate Love	Clare Chamberlain	17
Easter Sonnet	Michael R Collings	18
The Easter Month	Dominic James	19
Triumphant Over Death	Don R Wilkins	20
Awakening	Ted Pryor	21
Easter	Evelyn Leite	22
Easter Garden	David Sewell Hawkins	23
Born Again	Margaret Thompson	24
Jesus	Joan Hands	25
Easter Inspirations Poem	Claudete Carby	26
New Life	Paul Green	27
Resurrection Day	Renelle L Hall	28
Easter Service	Stephen Eric Smyth	30
Easter	Marian Bythell	31
Sure	Patricia Lewis	32
Easter Time	Ian Godfrey	33
The Cross	Ntamack Serge	34
Garden Of Peace	Rebecca Guest	35
Blacksheep	K Rawstron	36
Good Friday	Brian Muchmore	37
The Deal	Anthony M McCarrey	38
Spring's Risen Arms	Rozanna Alfred	39

Title	Author	Page
The Unifying Light	T J Dean	40
Winter Challenges Holy Earth	P Carleton	41
To The Slaughter Thy Lamb	Mark Anthony Noble	42
Spring	Sharyn Waters	43
Easter	I G Corbett	44
Chocolatier	Anya Lees	45
Easter (2004)	Christopher Major	46
Easter Should Be Fun	Hannah Wells	47
Sunny Good Friday	John F King	48
Easter Inspiration	Gael Nash	49
The Easter Daffodils	David J C Wheeler	50
The Legend Of The True Cross	Jackie Hinden	51
Easter Today	Sylvia Goodman	52
First Easter	Arthur Pickles	53
After The First Good Friday	Marjorie Piggins	54
Spring Thoughts	Rita E Sturdy	55
A Step Into Spring	Helen Kemp	56
Flowers	Ben Henderson Smith	57
Easter 2003	Margaret Ann Wheatley	58
The Way Home	Jean Bloomer	59
Pilgramage	Jane Ward	60
Death Could Not Hold Him	Jane Clay	61
Emmaus	Rosemary Keith	62
Son Of God	Pauline Bloomfield	64
Easter	Pearl Devereux	65
What Does Easter Mean To You?	Eileen Price	66
Resurrection	John Rowland	67
The Crown Of Thorns	Nadine Garrod	68
Spring Has Come	Veronica E Terry	70
Eternal Renewal	Catherine Rothman Le Dret	71
Rise In The East	M C Jones	72
Murderous Legacy	Frank Littlewood	73
Easter	Jack Scrafton	74
The Road To Easter	Edith Buckeridge	75
Night Nurses	John C Jordan	76
Easter	M Wilcox	77

Title	Author	Page
A Moment In Time	Joan Thompson	78
The Calvary Cross: An Ode To Jesus	Andrew Banks	79
Easter Sunday	Carole A Cleverdon	80
A Thought At Easter	Sheila Redpath	81
The Easter Egg	Hazel George	82
Love Unending	Alwyn Wilson	83
The Meaning Of Easter	Thelma Cook	84
I Am The Way	Sean O'Kane	85
God's Garden	Lorna June Burdon	86
Easter	J M Stoles	87
Easter Time	Maggie Strong	88
The Joy Of Easter	Gordon Forbes	89
Easter Time	Winifred Shore	90
The Swing	Bernard Brady	91
Easter	Nathan Luetchford	92
Easter Is Here	Geoff Vineall	93
God Loves Us	Ogbodo John Obinna	94
It Is Finished	Mike Clifford	95
Easter Thoughts	Jenny Stevens	96
Easter Vigil	Susan Latimer	97
Easter Time	E Saynor	98
Life's Triumph	V E Godfrey	99
A Beloved Child	D Carne	100
A Thought Of Spring	Joan Taylor	101
John 19:19	Olliver Charles	102
Messiah	Catherine E Atkinson	103
The Third Day (II)	Helen Thorn	104
Easter Inspirations	Dora L Stuart	106
Easter Meditation	Diana Lynch	107
The Meaning Of Easter	John Goodspeed	108
The Heavens Wept	Patricia Adele Draper	109
Easter Reflections	Peggy Courteen	110
Easter	Ian Tiso	111
Easter 2000	Steve Glason	112
Pieta	Jane England	113
Easter Remembered	Tim Nice	114
Judas	Chris Sherlock	115

Sunlit Garden	Jo Lee	116
Easter	Doreen Petherick Cox	117
Easter Promise	Greta Gaskin	118
Palms Of Jericho	Christopher Payne	119
The Joy Of Easter	Marjorie Picton	120
Sad	Cassy Bailey	121
New Life	Maryska Carson	122
Jesus: A Prayer To Himself	Matteo Sedazzari	123
Easter	Bernadette Woehrle	124
An Easter Recipe	Sarah Dodds	125
Chicken Or The Egg	Neil West	126
Easter Time	Ben Wilkinson	127
INRI (Jesus Nasarenus Rex Judaeorum)	Ntamack Serge	128
From Obscurity Into The Light	Ann G Wallace	129
Royal Colours	Kathleen M Hatton	130
Blooming World	J Evans	131
Easter Christening	Leigh Crighton	132
The Crowned Prince Of Earth	Julia Pegg	133
Easter And Springtime	Carol Ann Darling	134
Chocoholic	Gillian Humphries	135
Love Beyond Our Measure	Stuart Wood	136
Reawakening	Norman Bissett	137
For Me	Adedotun Adejuyigbe	138
Jesus Is Lord	Deirdre Banda	139
In Praise Of Easter	Sandra J Walker	140
The Forgotten Easter	Kathleen Townsley	141
The Glory Of The Easter Story	Rose Vincent	142
Lament In Resurrection	David McDonald	143
An Easter Dawn	Paul McLynn	144
Easter Is Here!	Duncan Catterall	145
Easter Music	Clare Dawson	146
Easter Resolution	P K Janaky	147
An Easter Prayer	Mary Hughes	148

A Springtime Morning

The music of the wildlife breaks the silence and the calm,
With sheep and horses grazing in this field with no alarm,
The vibrant colours blooming from the ground beneath my feet,
This crisp clear springtime morning is a sight you will not beat.

Above, the rays of sunshine glitter through the clouds that pass,
The breath of lifeless breezes, just disturb the blades of grass,
The sky, a vast blue blanket, yes so pure and so clean,
It's such a perfect contrast to the scenery of green.

This day makes me appreciate, to stop and spare a thought,
That life it is a miracle, however long or short,
Yes on a special day like this, these things I love so much,
The senses we were born with, that is hearing, sight and touch.

The pleasant sounds of nature, softly ringing in my ears,
The lambs are bleating constantly, no need for them to fear,
The humming of the bluebirds and the buzzing of the bees,
And chirping of the sparrows that are nesting in the trees.

To see displays of dewdrops sparkle like a precious stone,
Surrounded by a presence, so I know I'm not alone.
The rustle of the branches as the passing wind does kiss
I thank God for these senses, which without these things I'd miss.

A bitter cold bright morning, I can feel it on my face,
I come here to relax it's true, a peaceful, tranquil place
This world is full of beauty it's not difficult to find,
A special springtime morning, is so gentle, calm and kind.

Robert Basham

EASTER CHANGES

When I was young in '23
Easter was a holiday -
For some, but never one for me.
It was a very busy day.

Three times I went to church to ring
The bells. Then in the choir to sing.
The afternoon to Sunday School,
Teaching boys the golden rule!

When sent to London, knew no one,
So Easter found me all alone,
With nothing but the streets to roam
I caught the first train back to home.

Then came the war, with Easter just another day,
When everyone would only pray
For bombs and doodle-bugs to stray
And blow-up somewhere far away!

Now in old age - how time does go,
I'm given an Easter egg to show,
Then hear it on the radio,
But otherwise, would never know!

Walter Dalton

EASTER IN SCOTLAND 2002

Speckled in the distance
pale heathery children
tear through brambles

As I amble closer
they tumble down slopes
collapsing with laughing
pinched, peachy faces
gazing skyward.
As chocolatey fingers
linger on their lips,
silvered paper
keeps the rest for later
after the picnic.

Audrey Marshall

EASTER MORNING, BALLYCULTER

As is his won't on Easter morn
The Rector in a voice forlorn
With solemn face and watery eye
Reminds us all that we must die,
And yet, whatever he may say,
New life, not death, redeems this day.

High in the roof, a nesting dove
Croons in a sensuous voice of love.
A dusty sunbeam filtering through
Illuminates an empty pew.
(The congregation much prefer
To choose the pews towards the rear).

From cottage plot and sheltered hedge
To altar cloth and window ledge
The primrose and the daffodil
In earthen pot and milk jug fill
The shadowed nave with golden light
All dewdrop fresh and Easter bright.

The village folk and farmers sing,
The Easter alleluia's ring
Across the churchyard daffodils.
Cupped in the hollow of the hills,
This church stands, country deep, serene,
Amongst the shades of gold and green.

Like blessings on the world below,
The daffodil and primrose grow
Outside the darkened screen of yew,
Hiding from vulgar public view
The family gravestones of the Wards,
The Bangor ladies and their lords.

The Stockdales, Presses, Mrs Lunn
File past the Rector, one by one;
The Jacksons, Johnstons, Quails and Creas,
McKibbin kids with winsome ways,
And round brown eyes and dimpled smiles
Tip-tupping down the emptying aisles
And down the lane on dancing legs
To Sunday lunch and Easter eggs.

Beyond the sea, the hills of Man
The distant blue horizon span.
The bitter winds of winter passed,
Spring's blessing on the land at last.
The newborn lambs, the calves at play
And I rejoice this Easter day.

John Potter

IN PAMPHILL WOOD (DORSET)

A beautiful tranquil
hidden wood,
Where all bluebells are
proudly stood.
Underneath the darkened
damp trees
The toadstools catching
your eyes with glee!
Colourful primroses
delight you as you move away.
The birds twitter in hedges
with a lot to say,
Then, I wandered out onto the
meadow grass
And through a swinging gate
at last!
To remember the green and purple
in this enchanting place which is
always at hand.

Sammy Michael Davis

EASTER

Easter Sunday, chocolate eggs abound
Family, you've not seen in a while come round,
Celebrations bringing folk together again,
A few beers and a bar-b and usually rain!

What is it with Easter that brings such rapport?
A time to reflect maybe, of what went before.
The Son of God, Jesus, He died for our sin
He carried the burden for you and your kin.

He meant no one harm, this mild-mannered soul
A messenger of peace with the ultimate goal
To rid the world of everything wrong
Spreading His word, through prayer and in song.

Alas it wasn't to be, and such was our loss,
When Good Friday came, He was nailed to a cross
Women wailed and grown men cried
Jesus Christ, their Saviour had died.

It was Easter Sunday, when God claimed His son
He rose from His tomb amidst rays of the sun
One day He'll return, when peace reigns supreme,
Until then enjoy Easter and your eggs filled with cream.

Chris Thomas

EASTER

I will be remembered
My hour, short and sweet
I carried the Saviour
Palms strewn round my feet.

I grew as a tree
And then was chopped down
To make a sad cross
In place of a crown.

I've been here forever
A cave, dark and wide
I held the Saviour
Yes! 'Twas Jesus who died.

I ponder these happenings,
Was all this for me?
For a poor wretched sinner
He was nailed to a tree.

Now let's sing with gladness
Today Jesus lives
So we'll live forever
All our sins He forgives.

Beryl Van Donk

AN UNLUCKY BREAK

There was a snooker tournament for players who were small,
You had to be, for this event, no more than four feet tall.

A lower table it was got, so players they could see
Whene'er they wished to play a shot; or tricky that might be!

The Rest (for long shots), normally is placed the table under.
The ref protested formally that this would be a blunder.

For as the ref was six feet eight, 'twould wreck his back and chest,
To have to stretch beneath the slate each time they used the Rest.

The powers that be, they did agree, at end of lengthy talk
To place the Rest an inch or two above the players' walk.

When Scotland Yard did spot this lapse, it showed a slight concern,
And sent two undercover chaps to see what they could learn.

Now, as the first small man to play, (a man from Argentina),
Did pass below where Rest did lay, police approached arena.

Now what d'you think police applied - could you, I wonder a-guessed?
Two handcuffs, as they loudly cried, 'Don't move!
                                         You're under a Rest!'

Alan Dudeney
(The Poet Laurie-ate-for tea)

WORDS FROM THE CROSS

'I thirst! I thirst!' the Saviour cried,
As on the cross He hung.
'I thirst! I thirst!' He cried again -
Till someone came and offered
Him a drink.
But He refused and turned His head
Knowing they did not understand -
His thirst to do the Father's Will!
'I thirst! I thirst!' He cried again
Then Jesus bowed His head -
Crying 'It is finished!'
Knowing now He had fulfilled -
His Father's Will!

Christina Miller

MULTIPLICATION

The seasons change and spring has come
It's lovely to feel the warmth of the sun
The birds are bursting into song
Nests full of eggs and some with young
Busy bees are buzzing and all the trees are budding
Bursting with new foliage herbs of
Rosemary, thyme and sage
The sweetest smells fill the air
As all in nature display their wares
As from the winter blues we rise
It feels so good to be alive
There is no reason to wonder why
Everything alive wants to multiply.

A Wilcox

APRIL DAY

The sun is alive
And springs down through
The crystal shine of the water.
Berries sway, the sky deep awake
With our fantasies.

Though I can't quite put my finger
On why the myriad shades
And scents and hazy sounds,
Should ever be endowed
With such love for me.

David Mitchell

EASTER

Stop holding your breath
I have returned
(As you knew I would)
New dawn uncovers the cage
Releasing birdsong
Buds burst
Dewponds writhe
I have arrived
Survived
Life renewed
I celebrate
Splashing green and yellow
Across the hope-filled earth

Alex O'Grady

EASTER FOR ME (I)

Have you ever thought it through
What Easter really means to you?
It's not about Easter eggs or the Easter bunny
Or a period in the calendar we'd rather forget in a hurry

Easter is no ordinary time
If we'd just stop to think we'd soon realise
It's a story about the greatest rescue
How one man became our substitute

A death we all would have faced
Had He not taken our place
His sacrifice as an atonement for sin
Kept open (for us) the doors to eternity with Him

Our salvation hanged in the balance with this 'Man of Galilee'
The destiny of the world, the fate of humanity
He could have left us to perish in our iniquity
Remember His prayer, 'Father, if it be possible, let this cup pass
                                                    from me'
(Matt 26:39)

And later with a loud voice He did cry
'E'-li, E'-li, la'-ma sa-bach'-tha-ni?' (Matt 27:46)
Christ chose, consented to bear this burden of guilt
Praying, 'Nevertheless not as I will, but as thou wilt' (Matt 26:39)

Easter is about Christ suffering
And yet more, it is everything!
It exposes the depths to which God was willing to go to save man
It moves us as nothing else can

Calvary constitutes the most expensive price ever paid for anything
That God's love for man cost Him everything

We may take God for granted in what we do
And He may not feature in the plans of me and you
But on the cross He showed humanity
Without Him there is no you and me

Delroy Dwyer

EASTER IS HERE

Easter is here
the bunny has come
and fun is near
the egg hunt's begun

Look under the mat
and inside the drawer
there's one in the hat
let's find some more

There's some in the yard
and behind a blind
this is getting hard
there's no more to find

There's one on the ground
in the clover
all of them are found
the egg hunt is over

Ashleigh Rice (11)

CHOCOLATE LOVE

What do you remember
At Easter time?
Would it be chocolate?
Presents and wine?

Could it be bunnies?
Cute as can be,
Can't twitch his nose,
At you and me.

Brown chocolate, white chocolate
It is that time of year
Mounds of chocolate
Easter is here.

Could it be chickens?
Caught in the sun,
Gold wrapping paper
But they can't run.

Could it be Easter eggs?
Tasty to some,
Always competing
'Gainst the hot cross bun.

Could it be Jesus?
From Heaven above
For He died on a cross
So have faith in His love.

It's about love and hope,
In case your forget,
Remember Jesus,
Not just chocolate.

Clare Chamberlain

Easter Sonnet

When Earth is casketed by sombre snow
And winter's caging strength strains to its height,
Then winds like lengths of sun-warmed satin blow,
And thawing rivers shiver in skittish flight;

When barren mountains seem most bare,
And plains in fallow soil lie dressed,
Then greening, swelling buds appear
And silent grove to rustlings press;

When sparrows refuse to sing,
And lilies hide their hue,
Then man-song takes wing,
Earth breathes life renewed.

And all the world of life revels in spring,
To celebrate eternal Christ, life's King.

Michael R Collings

THE EASTER MONTH

Winter fuelled by starlight
Is the debt of thought to night,
When spring arrives it first returns
Astronomers' Narcissi
And daffodil reflections
In the colours of the sun,
Rich yolk, face among flowers,
The time moves on, impeachable,
We gain a year and lose an hour
And close the book on wisdom.

If snow falls in the Easter month
It dwindles into birdsong,
The anguish of recovery
Accelerates from tree to man
In a day, this time of year,
In deftly perfumed seconds,
The world invokes a wisdom
Better than of thought itself,
In our time we blossom fair
To broach the heat of summer.

Dominic James

TRIUMPHANT OVER DEATH

Word by Spirit was sent forth;
accomplish virgin birth.
Bring hope to the hearts of those
who suffer spirit dearth

Child of Mary, not birthday by man,
but by the spirit came.
He was the Son of God, it's said;
Jesus was His name

He dwelt in Earth, His only cause,
to do the Father's will.
This Word still echoes o'er the years,
for men to do this still.

The garden was His final trial,
for there He knew His fate.
Gave His will to Father's hand,
stood to meet men's hate.

On the cross His passion shown,
that all men should be free.
Forgave His foes, to Father said;
my spirit give to Thee.

By Father's will from death arose.
Triumphed o'er the grave.
Seated now at God's right hand,
all mankind to save.

Don R Wilkins

AWAKENING

Canterbury-blue sky;
wind-tossed clouds;
rough-skinned oaks;
soft-sighing boughs -
awakening to the call of spring.

Artesian-blended river;
green-clad banks;
purple-hued blossoms;
sleep-filled buds -
awakening to the kiss of life.

Daffodil-yellow heads;
slender-green stems;
silent-bluebell chimes;
pink-soaked petals -
awakening to nature's love.

Pollen-rich air;
nectar-sweet gifts;
feet-flattened paths;
wonder-filled thoughts;
and dreams of delight
awakening in children's minds.

Ted Pryor

EASTER

Watch with me as the wind an awesome vigil
keeps and sweeps the trees with blossoms
bending, white and waiting like an Earth
delivering in immortal splendour
all the glory of the risen Christ.

Hear the empty waiting in the closing tomb
of night, the half-beat hearts, the stifled
breath upon the bloodless form unseen,
hear whispered wisdom strengthening
the hours before the life-renewing morn.

Share with me the treasures of a life
transformed with love that reaches depths
of sadness, comforts pain, shelves empty
needs and selfish deeds, instils in each
His gifts of patience, joy and peace.

Evelyn Leite

EASTER GARDEN

Mary stealing at first light
Comes to Joseph's garden-tomb,
Filled with love and tears and fright.

Rough-hewn boulder sealed the night,
Now, pale shades begin to loom,
Mary stealing at first light.

Ointment to embalm, clutched tight,
Mary carries through the gloom,
Filled with love and tears and fright.

She has no strength nor men's might
To roll the rock from the tomb,
Mary stealing at first light.

No need now! New life and bright
Dawns on her penumbral rheum,
Filled with love and tears and fright.

The gardener's voice brings delight
To sad eyes of pendant doom
When Mary steals at first light,
Filled with love and tears and fright.

David Sewell Hawkins

BORN AGAIN

You were born in spring time
When new life all around
Was nesting in the treetops
Stirring under ground
You were washed by April rain
Warmed by morning sun
I saw you take your first steps
Watched you leap and run
Knowing you were special
As apon this Earth you trod
Born again at Easter
To be the lamb of God

Margaret Thompson

JESUS

I knew Him well
He comes to me
When I am sad inside
Grieving for a friend or foe
He lets me see
His divinity
Not the thing called sin
The thorns He wore
I would bear for Him.
In endless time He changes not
I love Him so much
He is my friend, adviser too
And it is true
I want to shout
That He is near
Nearer than a whisper in my ear
All the doubts and sadness goes
Surrounds me with goodness
As His love flows.

Joan Hands

EASTER INSPIRATIONS POEM

When I think of Easter
This is what I see
Shrubs and flowers in bloom
The smell of sweet scents fills the room

Easter is a time for all things new
And those that are religious, there are quite a few
Who go to church and praise His name
In other countries they do the same

Easter is a time of four seasons in one
Lambs are out to pasture
Walks are lovely this time of year
To keep in touch with nature

Spring is in the air
Baby chicks are born
Easter bunnies too
This is such a wonderful time for folks like me and you

Claudete Carby

NEW LIFE

This is the season of new life
Baby lambs
Beautiful flowers
New life fills the fields
We also remember
What Jesus
Did
The pain and terror
He took
So that I'd live forever
But not even
Death could hold Him
So we remember
Jesus rose
He's alive

Paul Green

RESURRECTION DAY

Mary and Mary at the tomb
Come to see where they had laid the Lord
The dawning of the third day
His death had pierced them as a sword

An earthquake - the stone was rolled away
An angel with countenance as lightning
The keepers became as those who're dead
Oh, hear what words as they ring . . .

Fear not, I know ye seek Jesus,
He is not here - He is risen as He said.
Come see - The place where the Lord lay.
Go tell - His disciples He's not dead!

He is risen - He's alive!
He is risen - The King for evermore
He is risen - He's alive!
He is risen - Salvation, it is sure!

He's alive . . .

When you take this bread, remember me
When you take this cup, remember my blood spilt for you.
Take heed you do not so unworthily
Search your hearts again anew

The love of the Lord is unlimited
By human thought or human word
There's more than enough for whosoever will
Even now, His gospel, it is heard!

Born, grown, a minister to sinful men
Died on a wicked cross for all
Taking the penalty for all our sin
Believe and receive Him as He calls -

As He calls -

Renelle L Hall

EASTER SERVICE

A tiny spark fumbled to an ordered flame;
one candle lit, then once and twice
proclaimed by solemn voice.
The fire links out
spread candle to candle
widening in hearthy ripple.
Expectant eyes glinting and cheeks Rembrandted
the community crackles and breathes anew.
The voice intones once more:
Hope. Hope. Hope.

Stephen Eric Smyth

EASTER

Easter blessings come your way
For Friday, Saturday and Sunday
Chocolate eggs and hot cross buns
Remembering Jesus, Holy Son.

Marian Bythell

SURE

Listen. Hear my heartbeat
faint as the scuff of slack rain
on falling leaves. Be sure
that it echoes the chafe of death.
Already the dark earth is runnelled;
it bleeds like shadow in low sun.

Be sure that time will unravel
skeins of grief. Let their threads
swirl around your heart.
The earth will not sleep
but will merely drowse,
awaiting spring's first glint.

And as sure as spring will succour
starved hillsides, as sure
as she will flesh the ribs of stark trees
so will she breath on me
with breath warmed by spools of sunlight
she has loosed.

Be sure that I will smile again, laugh again,
will grieve, feel pain and weep again.
Be sure that I will love again.
And that my love will be steadfast
as the seasons' faithful chant,
be sure.

Patricia Lewis

EASTER TIME

For some, Easter is a time
For hot cross buns
For eggs in colour
For chicks in the runs.
For eating simnel cake
For lambs in the field
For rabbits on the make.

For some, Easter is a time
For fresh daffodils
For bonnet parades
For catching spring chills.
For school holidays
For time off work
For jammed motorways.

For some, Easter is a time
For stirring from stupor
For planting of crops
For preparing the future.
For cleansing one's soul
For renewing of hope
For charting one's goal.

For some, Easter is a time
For exchanging greetings
For affirming one's faith
For special church meetings.
For praising God's Son
For giving Him thanks
For all He has done.

For me, Easter is a time
For chocolate.

Ian Godfrey

THE CROSS

My people are crying
I have just one handkerchief
My people are hungry
I have just one slice of bread
My people are thirsty
I have just one glass of water
My people are sick
I'm just a little doctor
My people call out: help me
I'm just a man but not a God

Ntamack Serge

GARDEN OF PEACE

So peaceful here with the outer world blocked out,
Yet calming comfort in the fact that it is everywhere.
The little noises become intensely magnified,
As the deafening roar of traffic sinks into the background.
The building's beauty become highlighted by the distance,
As people sit watching the world go slowly by.
The seconds melt into hours, as the hours melt into being,
People in no hurry by the ticking clock.
The garden smells fresh and new with life,
No world of pressure existing within.

Rebecca Guest

BLACKSHEEP

Eloi, Eloi, lama sabachthani?
'My God, my God, why have you forsaken me?'
The cry of the blacksheep,
Suffering the ultimate disgrace -
Separation from the Father.

The Son of the Father, the pure-bred white sheep,
Perfect, without stain or blemish,
Took the place of the blacksheep -
My place, your place,
Suffering 18-certificate violence,
Beaten to a pulp, an utter mess,
And died like a common criminal.

The pure, white sheep paid the ultimate sacrifice,
Taking on our blackness
And turning it white -
Clean, pure, spotless,
So we could be accepted into the family fold.

K Rawstron

GOOD FRIDAY

Why call today *Good* Friday? The day that Jesus died,
nailed upon a wooden cross, till, in despair He cried,
'Father, have you forsaken me? If so, please tell me why?'
With that last call, the deep was done, it seemed the end was nigh.
They took his body from the cross, to where a cave, blocked by a stone,
had been loaned, by one who cared. He'd prepared it for his own.
The body, wrapped in shrouds of white, anointed first with balm,
was laid inside, past earthly care, no more could come to harm.
His weeping friends then left Him there, and went away to mourn.
They'd find no peace of mind that day, or sleep before the dawn.
Their friend was dead and buried now; they'd lost their leader too,
should they return to homes and kin? What else was left to do?
So, why call this day, Friday - *Good,* when all that occurred was bad,
with fear and pain, and finally death, and people, oh so sad?
Through Saturday they stayed and talked, about the bloody deed.
They talked and talked, all through the night. Oh how their hearts
                                                                did bleed.
Then came the end to that long night. The first *Easter Sunday morn.*
Time to leave the one they loved, and start to make for home.
'I must just say goodbye to Him,' one said, Mary was her name.
So, to the cave she made her way, but then - 'twas not the same.
The stone was gone, placed there by ten, but now - just cast aside.
As she drew near, no corpse she saw, an empty tomb she spied.
A figure then, she saw ahead. 'Where have you laid Him - please?'
The man just turned, held up his hand, said, 'Mary - be at ease.'
With heart so full of love and joy, back to their friends she sped.
To tell the great and wondrous news, how swift that news then spread.
It's spread and spread, two thousand years that is, less twenty-one.
Jesus was dead - but now *He lives. He is the Father's Son.*

So that is why, Good Friday's *good. Christ* triumphed over death.
He died that we, like *Him,* might live, and breathe, again, *God's* breath.

Brian Muchmore

The Deal

So glad he sees my point of view,
He thought,
Reaching for the salt.
So very sensible of you!
He smiled across the table.
After all . . .
They'll only ask him questions,
Nothing much . . .
Then pack him back up north
As soon as they are able.
And he'll be safe and free,
And we'll have thirty silver pieces -
Splendid!

The other eyed him, sadly.
'Go on,' he said,
'Do what you have to do.
Let's have an end to it.'

Anthony M McCarrey

SPRING'S RISEN ARMS

Spring embraces me -
I lie on a soft green pasture
I see spring lambs graze in leisure
- in awe of a lamb's docility to be
sacrificed on the bare cross for me
Oh, spring awakens mystical history
unveiling to me a paschal mystery

Spring blossoms in my heart -
dawning of light on a spring's eve
with shedding of last evergreen leaf
- was naked, cold as a shivering oak
till spring clothes me, flowering hope
Oh, spring's morn of unstained birth
after a winter's night of stained death

Spring fills the abyss of my soul -
to lily white pureness, rain washes me
prejudiced nailed, resurrects new me!
- serenity prayer fills, a serene sense
spring's breath of sweet frankincense
Oh, winter's penury fades out to let in
spring's riches of hues, songs to set in

Spring unburdens my laden core
like rosy apples harvested of a laden
bough - hope sodden heart, gladden
- I come, come to bear fruits of piety
for spring has brought me gifts aplenty
Oh, embracing me - God's risen arms
as I lie on the pasture reciting psalms.

Rozanna Alfred

THE UNIFYING LIGHT

Following every dark night there rises a brighter dawn,
So Good Friday is the prelude to Easter morn.
When the Son of God by sacrificing His life for sins of others,
Became the Risen Christ, binding us together as sisters and brothers.
So in prayer as one family we should all unite,
For though there are many paths, there is only one light.

T J Dean

WINTER CHALLENGES HOLY EARTH

I will search you out with accusing fingertips,
Cross dark continents with flood after fire.
I will give you haunting, unearthly melodies
Plucked from nature's most eerie of choirs.

I shall possess your days and plunder your nights,
Mocking your name on the calling wind.
I shall be proud earth's tormentor,
Forcing to flight, fragile migrating wings.

You will command me to leave your earthly dominion,
Carrying with me the shrouds of my dead.
You will pray for Holy Earth's resurrection.
Awaiting new life to surge from those who have bled.

P Carleton

TO THE SLAUGHTER THY LAMB

Momentarily envision the face of starvation
On a child in the dirt of the road
Where he begs
For the price of a meal
His salvation
If only but more
Be the use of his legs
The treatment for which
Costs considerably less
Than one of your chocolatised eggs

As you gorge you indulge in decreasing your faith
Increase you your sins, unleash you your fate
Gormandising whilst others so suffer
Be surely something
That Jesus would hate
Whatever your ruling on Christ
Be it known that no perfect
A person be since
For He died in the midst of a people
Who of deliverance remain unconvinced

In the essence of Easter
Be the presence of God
And whatever that presence portrays
'Tis a time to draw close to your maker
Pay homage, repent, and give praise
To reflect on the doings
Of a lamb to the slaughter
That His trials in life forever remain
Diving He, or righteously flawless
Designed He, to spare you, from ever His pain

Mark Anthony Noble

SPRING

S eason when bulbs begin to shoot
P urple, yellow, white crocuses
R abbits with their kittens looking very cute
I adore the spring it's so fresh, so green
N ature's living beauty
G ardens dressed in a variety of colours an image of
a wonderful scene

Sharyn Waters

EASTER

Easter symbolises the heart
Of the Christian faith
Christ gave His life, for all
He carried the weight
Of the sins, of the world
By death, upon the Cross, on Good Friday
To rise in glory, on Easter morn
On the Cross, at Calvary
His end, was not to be
He gave His life, for all to see
In the garden, at Gethsemane
On Easter Sunday morn
The Christian faith, was born
We celebrate, Christ's
Risen life anew
With fresh life, all around
The Easter lily, first flower
Christ did see, in the garden on Easter morn
Fresh flowers, fresh buds, spring anew
Church bells ring, Christians sing
Christ the Lord is risen, today
Hallelujah, hallelujah!
The stone was rolled away,
This is Easter day! Rejoice!

I G Corbett

CHOCOLATIER

My life is like chocolate
Sometimes white, sometimes milk, at times even plain or dark
It can come in sprinkles or chips, lightly topping off
To large heavy slabs, crashing down.
It's always there, but not always eaten,
Maybe just hidden in a cupboard, or stored in a drawer
Waiting to be acknowledged, picked up and used
Too much and it can make you sick
It can be melted down or frozen at any point
We can bite it, suck it, taste it with just a lick
We never realise how much we adore it until it's gone.
We know it won't last but we still want more, hold on
We abuse it when we're down or sad
Not everyone enjoys it, and some choose to give it away
Either way, behind my burst of cravings - good or bad
I know I have control until my melt-down day.

Anya Lees

EASTER (2004)

The load was very heavy,
you needed help to carry the frame;
and how you struggled
when the metal pierced your hands.
While you flinched,
the sign above your head
told why you were there -
DIY supastore
Spend less, get more.

Christopher Major

EASTER SHOULD BE FUN

It was Easter sixty-eight
The one I remember most
I was standing by the gate
Whiter than a ghost

I wish Easter made me smile
Like most people will
Even for a while
No warmth, just a chill

Good Friday was so sunny
The Saturday was blue
Sunday wasn't funny
Monday hurt too much to be true

My siblings all got eggs
I remember oh so well
Where was mine I asked him
I'd been a good girl

I stood at that gate
A tear in my eye
It grew dark, it grew late
I'd given up asking why

Not a happy Easter tale
I'm very sad to say
And in this I'll never cease to fail
But in God I'll find a way . . .

Hannah Wells

SUNNY GOOD FRIDAY

Some roads are lined with Hibiscus
Others with thorns.
Some you can read on the map
And you make all the right connections -
It really is no trouble at all.
Some are long, some wide,
The difference may not be as important as you imagine.
The unfamiliar road as difficult as the one you knew well.

John F King

EASTER INSPIRATION

Easter, a time of reflection and meditation
Of mixed messages, mixed emotions
The dark dense gloom of Good Friday
The death of Christ, carrying the burdens of the world
The three hours of intense sorrow and pain
As He watched humanity at His feet.
The explosion and intensity of joy as the tomb burst forth.
Easter Sunday, a day of celebration
New life, new vision, new hope.
The warmth of the sun arousing the sleeping
The gentle breeze of spring arousal
Awakening life in the freshness of flowers
The verdant green of newly mown grass
Dew sparkling on yellows and pinks in dappled light
Sap rising and a quickening of the spirit.
Our son went missing on Maundy Thursday
In the depths of the Atlantic
Wrecking his life and leaving a shell
In the cavernous deep
His body shackled to the ruins of his plane
But his soul released
He lives only in our hearts
This year, it falls on Good Friday
Renewal to us is pain
Memories exacerbated by Easter.
Yet clinging to faith, for fear of falling
God willing, an Easter in the future
Will bring us peace and thanksgiving
For the one who has departed
And is safe in the hands of God.

Gael Nash

THE EASTER DAFFODILS

With Easter late, the daffodils
    are dying where they once stood tall,
The golden heads are ragged now,
    and where the wind cuts chill, some fall,
Yet in the flowers' wilting hearts
    are seeds of life which, if allowed,
One day, with trumpets of their own,
    will burst from winter's misty shroud . . .

In Jesus' death are seeds of life
For all who see, accept, believe.

Below the ground the bulbs lie hid,
    fed by their leaves' untidy green,
'Til that too dies, withers away,
    and we forget they've ever been,
Awaiting new life's urgent call,
    as Jesus' body, in the tomb,
Lay waiting for His Father's voice
    to change the grave into a womb . . .

In Jesus' resurrection, life
Is promised to all who'll receive.

The daffodils will soon be gone,
    their part played for another year,
As summer, autumn, winter flow,
    with time, o'er my perception's weir,
But Jesus, risen, glorified,
    no longer tied in time or space,
Will be my unseen Friend and Guide
    in ev'ry moment, ev'ry place . . .

In Jesus' life, my own from sin
I find the Living God retrieve.

David J C Wheeler

THE LEGEND OF THE TRUE CROSS

A piece of wood split into sufficient splinters
to plant a forest in Christendom -
a miracle, I suppose.

Does Christ care
what happened to that piece of wood?
Or that sea of sweat
poured into a thousand phials?
Or that piece of cloth which
some say carries
the imprint of his face?

What does it matter what Christ looked like?
Christians have sworn - haven't they? -
to forsake idols.

Miracles from bits of bone,
from smears of blood -
what has Christ to do with these?

We've wrapped him up
like a mummy, swathed
in grave clothes of superstition.

Christ lives! He broke free
from that mouldering shroud.
The only true legend is this.

Jackie Hinden

Easter Today

Where has it gone, the sorrow and the pain
That once was Easter?
Will its anguish and its joy not come again?

It seems the age has passed into the profane
And ever faster
We deride faith and eulogise the brain.

Few believers in religion now remain
Save in the cloister
Our age devoted most to commercial gain.

How many now in Lent truly abstain
And dwell on Easter?
We concentrate on food and the mundane

On chocolate eggs in foil and cellophane
Dietary disaster!
With hot cross buns and simnel cake explain

Stories the Bible told that appertain
To the great Pastor.
Rabbits, chicks and cards nowadays sustain

This season when the Godhead once was slain
That became Easter.
Yet there are still some who believe His reign

Continues even now and will regain
A brighter lustre
On earth and into the transmundane.

For faith is like a seed of hardy grain
To the great Master.
Burnt dry, it yields once more to mystic rain.

Sylvia Goodman

First Easter

He died alone:
Nailed to a Roman cross,
Nails driven -
Hammered into virgin flesh,
Blood . . . thorn inflicted
Trickled down into infinity
And across the space of time.

Soldiers gambled
Women wept
Men froze
Wind howled
Rain lashed
Heavens thundered
Innocent suffered -
A new age was born
As faith began its long
Journey to fulfilment.

Arthur Pickles

AFTER THE FIRST GOOD FRIDAY

Still - so still - for three long days,
The Earth, the sea, the sky,
No sound to break the silence
As the minutes laboured by,
But over all the smell of fear
From a world gone all awry.
Where was He now, their dearest Lord?
His disciples asked in vain.
Stiff in His tomb - His ministry done?
And there would He remain?
But Jesus had gone to help the dead,
And take away their pain.
In those three days, how Satan
Must have rubbed his hands in glee!
'He is dead! And I have triumphed!
The world belongs to me!'
But watchful in the heavens above
God saw His Son set His people free,
Salome and the two Marys
Crept out at break of day,
And found an angel guarding the open tomb,
He had rolled the stone away.
They could see their Lord was no longer there
And now they could not stay.
'Hosanna in the highest! The Lord is risen indeed!'
What cries - what shouts of triumph
From the people He has freed!
He is risen now in glory
With arms outstretched with love.
We'll be with Him soon in glory, high above.

Marjorie Piggins

Spring Thoughts

Hawthorn buds are bursting,
Snowdrops in full bloom,
Signs of winter's tight grip weakening;
High up in tall trees a woodpecker tapping constantly,
Crows fight noisily for the topmost branch.
On hidden islands swans will nest, safe from the wily fox,
Blackbirds begin to build their nests, above high banks
Clothed in primroses and violets so sweet;
Herons gather in their heronry high above the river;
A lone kingfisher swiftly crosses the river, a flash of iridescent blue;
Avenues of crocus bloom, a carpet of bright colour;
Soon bluebells will cover woodland floors, their colour quite unique
Blackbirds now sing their lay - spring has arrived at last!

Rita E Sturdy

A STEP INTO SPRING

Days are growing longer
As winter starts to fade
And healthy buds burst forth
To help the trees awake
Colours start appearing
Goodbye to shades of grey
When sun moves high above
And breezes blow the clouds away.

Daffodils sway gently
Magnolias pink and white
Tulips too coming forth
From their long winter sleep
Tight cupped shades of colour
How pretty they will be
Amongst the shades of green
With heads held high for all to see.

Lambs staying close to Mum
Their confidence lacking
Huddled against a fence
The wind still has a chill
As rainbows arch above
When sunshine follows rain
And Easter hymns ring out
To fill our hearts with joy again.

Helen Kemp

FLOWERS

Snowdrops in spring again,
Carnations following tulips coloured tall,
Daisies, a chain hanging her pretty neck circling,
And honeysuckle over the wall.
Bluebells a-carpeting,
Woods floor smoke covering,
Violets hiding shy,
Lilacs sweet scent spreading,
Foxgloves all a'tap'ring high,
And hollyhocks like beacons climbing,
Sunflowers sky highly grow,
Lupins, lighthouses glow,
Cowslips like yellow diamonds,
Forget-me-nots reflecting
Sparkling stars brightly shining,
Clover leaves cov'ring grass green grounds.
Sweet peas light petals dance
In colours various,
Marigolds hot summer sight,
Bees on each flower alight
To spread far and pollinate,
Ensuring coloured scents sweetly great
And I will give her roses far beyond compare,
Roses for the ev'ing, Royal roses for her hair.

Ben Henderson Smith

EASTER 2003

Indeed we do know
what prayer can achieve
and we are humbled.
Has ever this Christian time
seemed more relevant
or deeply part
of our lives
No one can fail
to be touched
by God's presence,
sharing in world events
close to our hearts
Loving, caring, praying and giving.

Margaret Ann Wheatley

THE WAY HOME

God knew our need
and sent His son
from home in Heaven
to live on Earth.

Human here, no home,
travelling light, free to roam.
His home was His heart
and He gave it to us.

New life He brought.
He came to save, to serve,
to love, to lead us
on the journey home.

Held in His hands
the life of the world.
Obedient to His Father
He died on a cross.

Heart wounded, work finished,
life given, journey ended,
He went home
to *His* Father.

The love, the triumph,
the promise, the hope.
Follow His footsteps home
to *our* Father.

Jean Bloomer

Pilgrimage

There's a hillside in Devon
That drops to the sea;
There's a plain wooden cross at the top;
Several people are sitting
In the soft evening sun
While lambs call in the valley.

We watch as the light
Becomes gold and then pink,
As the sun sinks into the sea,
And the cross grows dark
Etched against the sky,
Its outline and meaning stark.

We each have a stone
That means something to us
To lay at the foot of the cross
And one by one, in the quiet dusk,
We placed our meaning there,
A symbol of our trust!

I couldn't think of what to leave
In the beauty of that place,
Regret, or sin, or suffering
All needed the touch of God,
But only peace filled my soul
On this Easter hill,
So I laid my stone of love.

Jane Ward

DEATH COULD NOT HOLD HIM
(Reflections after a visit to the garden tomb, Jerusalem)

The tomb was truly empty,
Yet we felt that He was there,
His Spirit touched the grieving,
As we sat with them, believing
Those they loved were in His care.

The sun was warm upon us,
And the words of truth were said,
For His agony was real,
More than anything we'd feel,
Poured out wine and broken bread.

You, dear man, who brought the message,
Had just the week before,
Watched your mother go to Heaven,
Knowing all her sins forgiven,
Hope you brought, though still heartsore.

How you magnified our Saviour,
In that lovely, peaceful place,
Death, decay would never hold Him,
In His glory we'll behold Him
And, trembling at His brightness, see His face.

Jane Clay

EMMAUS

Enveloped in the ghostliness of dusk they traipsed
perturbed by queries, sifting the unknown
withdrawn through loss, their sights so low they failed
to see the one who paced with them until He spoke.

'What things were they discussing as they walked?
Was He the only one in town who had not heard?'
Why! All Jerusalem had been disturbed!
A mighty prophet both in deed and word

Jesus the Nazarene had been betrayed
and captured by our priests and rulers and
been crucified! Yet we had hoped that He would be
the Holy one of Israel come to set us free.

What's more at dawn this third day gone, some women
from our group had found His tomb was empty, save
for angels who appeared declaring that He lived!
Then others searched, but saw no sign of Him.'

'Oh foolish ones so slow to grasp all that
the prophets taught. Did you not know the Christ
must suffer unto death the tyranny of sin
to save mankind and then would rise in glory to His reign?'

Astounded by the stranger's rousing words
they fed like eager fledglings as he told God's plan
from ancient times to Moses, prophecies
and passages referring to the son of Man.

Their ears were tingling and their hearts aglow
they could not bear to let Him go and begged him stay
for it was 'getting dark', inspired uplifted now
as they had been in happier times before.

A simple meal prepared, their new friend raised the bread
and made a blessing which was quite unique -
His words transfixed, electrified, were known -
as out of dream theirs eyes were opened but their guest had flown.

Rosemary Keith

SON OF GOD

Of humble beginnings
came to Earth
through miraculous
virgin birth.

Treated with scorn
and treachery
yet He gave up
His liberty.

Healing, forgiving
then trustingly -
died on a cross
at Calvary.

He died for our sins
in utmost pain
look at the world,
did He die in vain?

Pauline Bloomfield

EASTER

Easter is a time for chocolatey fun,
Out bloom the flowers, in the spring sun,
Little bunny rabbits, hopping around,
Newborn lambs, jump and bound.

School is closed for the Easter break,
People on holiday, it is free time to take,
Families together, having lots of fun,
Now the better weather has finally begun.

Easter is the time for hope and of new living,
It is a time to enjoy and for new beginnings,
Apart from the fun what is Easter, what does it mean?
To remember Jesus Christ our Lord, who died for you and me.

Pearl Devereux

WHAT DOES EASTER MEAN TO YOU?

What does Easter mean to you?
Flying off to pastures new?
Traffic jams and airport queue?
Gardens bathed in spring-like hue?
Fluffy chicks, and choc-eggs, too?
Visits to friends, long overdue?
DIY shops, paint and glue?
Or taking the children to the zoo?
Easter to the godly few
Means check the service, fill the pew!
From a different point of view,
Lots of rest, methinks *I'm* due!
So, switch the phone off, you're all taboo,
Leave me be, till I feel new!

Eileen Price

RESURRECTION

Throughout the autumn, with its rainy gusts,
Old leaves stayed tight in the hedging beech.
No wind could hurl them to the garden's edge,
Nor thrust them into corners beyond my reach.

Then winter, with its fearsome gales and snow,
Tore at surrounding shrubs, relentless, no relief;
But still the beech held firmly to its coat,
Reluctant yet to yield a single dying leaf.

Snowdrops, gentle violets, nodding daffodils,
Appeared in turn within its rusting shade.
I watched the rabbits there, hungry for spring,
Even the field mouse scurried round and played.

But there, tight-furled on every ageing branch,
Small buds appeared; a sign of what will be.
Old leaves, new buds, living side by side,
Death and life together upon the tree.

The promised storm came on a Thursday night,
Fierce, and tearing every living thing.
It lasted through the night till Friday noon,
What destruction such a storm can bring!

And the beech, every ancient leaf was gone!
Then on Sunday, as the warm sun shone,
New leaves appeared, hope at length re-born.
The tree will live, to greet more joyful dawn.

John Rowland

THE CROWN OF THORNS

Who is this man who died for me?
This Son of God
With bowed head and tears of blood
That fall so silently
At my timid feet
I cannot look into His darkened eyes
As He hangs there in front of me
And I afraid
And insignificant

I sense His power
His love for me
Why is He hanging there
In front of me?
I look away, how could it be
That one so good
Died for me?

Dark clouds gather in the sky
The heavens roar,
It's time to die
To leave this earth
Where once He danced
Where just His smile left me entranced

The sight of Him
With crown of thorns
Embedded in His matted hair
Made me fall upon the ground
And look with a bewildered stare
I knew at last I'd found
Why He died for me
For insignificant me

I now can stand
With new life breathed into me
I sense His Presence ever near
His words, He whispers in my ear
Seek not for me
For I am here
I bring you peace
I set you free
And now I know
He died for me.

Nadine Garrod

SPRING HAS COME

Daffodils nodding in the wintry sun,
the scent of grass cuttings newly mown.
Blossom heavy on the waiting boughs.
Spring has come.

Yellow lambs' tails hanging low,
pussy willows soft as snow.
Evenings lengthening when the work is done.
Time for outings and family fun.
Spring has come.

Children laughing, sparkling eyes,
glimpses of blue in the showery skies.
Young lambs skipping, joyful leaps,
Mother calling with anxious bleats.
Hidden birds singing in lofty trees,
blossom drifting on the breeze.
Spring has come.

Planning holidays in the sun,
life is wonderful, winter's gone.
Breathe the air, forget your cares.
Spring has come.

Veronica E Terry

ETERNAL RENEWAL

Who are thee, nameless,
my beloved,
who urges in dark whispers
down the corridors of time?

Sibilant in the grasses
of winter's ending.
Staunch in rooted trees,
splendid in the river's winding,
the winds play thy harmonies.

Stare out the eager eyes
of childhood
and lie glorious in endless
fields of summer.

Howl with the moontides
ripped by Earth's ancient convulsions.
Caress the bride,
marry the groom,
carry off our sorrows
for the dead.

Thou, in pristine silence
are replete.
Sentient beyond time
life giving life,
wingtips of tender light,
without taste, the leavening.

Nowhere do I find thy form,
yet, I reach out
and touch always only thee.

Catherine Rothman Le Dret

RISE IN THE EAST

Sun in the sky,
will you dawn in the east,
show the world and wonder why,
daylight at the very least.

Dream on sunbeam,
shine like a light,
be my very sight,
will you rise again like Jesus Christ.

Soon in the noon,
you reach your highs,
blaze in the haze,
sunrise surprise.

I am cold,
your moving mountains to behold,
turn your skyward path,
bring shadows,
have your aftermath.

Set in the west,
as you leave these shores,
with red skies at the crests
of the waves of never more.

M C Jones

MURDEROUS LEGACY
(A less than holy reflection on the Easter story)

They told when I was a little lad
About a preacher cruelly crucified,
A horror story that, of course, they tried
To soften to my childish ears. He had
They said, worked miracles, restored the sick,
Raised people from the dead, and claimed He was
The Son of God, but met His death because
His words antagonised the priests, forever quick,
To stamp out rivals, yet could not resist
The growing faith their murderous crime unleashed.
However it occurred to me, the Christian priest
For many centuries on proved he'd not missed
Their methods and used all their gruesome tricks,
For getting rid of tiresome heretics.

Frank Littlewood

EASTER

It starts in darkness and despair,
With suffering, and with grief and loss,
All the world's sins are gathered there,
On that sad, silent, hopeless Cross.
Midst helplessness, and guilt, and shame
A vulnerable Saviour dies for us.
He dies in agony, grief and pain,
And no one cares, and there's no fuss.
He dies in love, our sins forgiven,
And hope restored to start anew.
To bring to Earth a taste of Heaven,
Its joy and freshness to endue.
The act is sealed on Easter Day,
And resurrection is the key,
New life bird, beast, and flower display,
As nature starts her springtime spree.
The air itself feels soft and light,
The sun sheds forth its stronger rays,
The Earth awakes, the scene is bright,
With rainbow colours all ablaze.
The season spreads its widening scope,
For Christ is risen, warmth returns,
New life abounds, with future hope,
And a new vigour in us burns.
But, best of all, the springtime brings
A promise in the burgeoning earth,
'Jesus lives!' the whole scene sings,
Announcing victory over death.

Jack Scrafton

THE ROAD TO EASTER

Shrove Tuesday we used all oddments
Ash Wednesday, the beginning of Lent
Forty days of giving something
Or forty days to live and repent

We may give up something we like
Or do good in so many new ways
Perhaps we'll reject chocolate
And not eat it for forty days

Helping others may give us cheer
If we see it makes them feel better
I am sure it gives them a glow
To greet them with cards or a letter

Soon it's Easter day with its joy
'Christ is risen' we all seem to sing
A happy day to celebrate
Rejoice now and hear the church bells ring

God's gift is done, and Jesus back
For now, and he stays here forever
To guard us and guide us each day
We pray that He will leave us never

Edith Buckeridge

NIGHT NURSES

They walk the silent ward at night
To keep the vigil lamp alight.
With touch and words of comfort spring
The medicines of hope they bring.
They answer to the patients' cries
And watch us with a thousand eyes.
Their selfless presence gentle, kind,
Fills every waking hour I find.
It is a long and ceaseless prayer
These duty hours when they are there.
But morning comes as time moves on
And like the night you too have gone.
Yet I have rued these many days
Since I left void of words of praise.
Two thousand years ago a Man
Showed us how love of neighbours can,
With thought and word and deed belaud
That vested, pious Lamb of God.
Yet I know that it has been said
The Lamb of God rose from the dead.
While His 'stone' had been rolled away
Upon that festive Easter day.
Now I here truly glorify
His precept I was counselled by.
It caused my 'stone' to roll away
To bring a peace this Easter Day.
Since we our different paths pursue,
My grateful thanks, long overdue.

John C Jordan

EASTER

Easter is approaching,
The eggs are in the shops,
And soon there will be children,
With chocolate on their tops.

The ladies on their diets,
Will find temptation hard,
When faced with gifts of chocolate,
If they let down their guard.

The lovers buy the naughty stuff,
That stays behind closed doors,
The dogs are followed on the scent,
With some stuck to their paws.

Ah, Easter is a special time,
That means so much to all,
A time to get together,
When friends and family call.

M Wilcox

A Moment In Time

What was it like for Mary
To see her dear Son die?
He was not the guilty one;
That was you and I.

She stood in the soaring Palestine heat
As the people scoffed and stared,
For six yours she watched His agony,
Was she the only one who cared?

Relatives and friends stood near her;
They too shared in her grief,
A soldier and one of the Sanhedrin,
Also a penitent thief.

This day was a moment in time;
From eternity He came,
To change the lives of all who believe,
In a world ne'er to be the same.

Joan Thompson

THE CALVARY CROSS: AN ODE TO JESUS
('People not yet born will be told, 'The Lord saved his people'. (Psalm 22.31)

Your bearded face
was beaten and battered and bruised.
Your sinewy carpenter's body
had been most cruelly used.

You saw Judas, your apostle,
a friend whom you would miss,
come up to you in the Garden
and betray you with a kiss.

You saw Caiaphas, the High Priest,
speak the words of condemnation,
and all the Sadducees and elders
give their vote of affirmation.

You saw Pilate, the Roman governor,
swallow the High Priest's lie,
then coolly sign the piece of paper
which said that You must die.

You were hung up on the Calvary Cross
enduring all the things you feared.
The scornful crowd on onlookers
laughed in Your face and jeered.

You saw your mother Mary
look upon You on the Cross
and bow her head in sorrow
overcome by her sense of loss.

Thus You hung on steadfastly
enduring all this strife.
Beaten and betrayed and cruelly used
still You remained the resurrection and the life.

Andrew Banks

Easter Sunday

The beauty of new life
Leaves pale as the spring day
Easter the time of rebirth

Jesus' resurrection both intertwined
The rebirth of trees and flowers
Jesus risen, hope at Easter time.

Carole A Cleverdon

A THOUGHT AT EASTER

Wandering into a world
Obscure and intransigent
I see wonders and beauties abound

Blinded by divergence
Deafened by egomania
It becomes an angelic sound

In the midst of violence
Down the road of oppression
Stop, think, look around

Famine and disaster besiege us
Disease and suffering overwhelm
Where can *he* be found?

See the kind heart selflessly given,
Hear the gentleness of whispered words,
Look to Jesu's suffering for each of us,
Through salvation and love we are crowned.

Sheila Redpath

THE EASTER EGG

When I was first created I was just a gooey mess
But then they put me in a mould and I started to impress!
First there were two halves of me sitting side by side,
But then they joined me in the middle, and I felt a sense of pride.

They started to adorn my body with a robe of pure tin foil
Then came the ribbons and the box so I was not to spoil
Next I had a journey, so I was packed within a lorry
I was leaving my birthplace now, so I felt a little sorry.

I was put high upon a shelf in a supermarket, this was the place to be,
And I was so impressed with all the goods that were surrounding me.
We were lined up like a regiment of soldiers standing in a row,
But this was not the place we had to stay, we knew we had to go.

To be sold it is a nice thing, but also hard to bear,
I had to leave my buddies on that shelf so I wiped away a tear.
But up until that point everything was seeming fine,
But then to my horror and dismay I met a boy of nine.

He had an evil glint within his eyes, when he first looked at me
He ripped the box, and laughed with pleasure as I became free
I saw his fist coming as he hit me to the ground,
I felt a little dazed as I was left in pieces all around.

The pain! Oh the pain, was indescribable as I lay upon the floor,
There was not an inch that I could feel that wasn't feeling sore.
But I thought that was the worst of it, but the worst was yet to come
As he put me in his mouth piece by piece and I slid down to his tum.

I will have to say this quick as there isn't much left for him to devour
I had a heart, and feelings, and this was meant to be my finest hour.
If you are brought an Easter egg, just remember me, and say *nooo*
Remember all this suffering, but now I have to *gooo* . . .

Hazel George

LOVE UNENDING

High up on that Cross
He had love on His face
His arms were outstretched
The whole world to embrace

The nails in His hands
And that crown of thorn
All these, and our sins
He had willingly borne

He asked for our forgiveness
But still we laughed and sneered
His pain it seemed unending
His side we even speared.

On that Cross Dear Saviour
For us Your life You gave.
The Lord of Heaven suffered
For even me to save.

Our Father, God of Heaven
Thank You for Your Son.
Through His death and resurrection
A victory He has won.

Alwyn Wilson

THE MEANING OF EASTER

Spring in the air, when all things come alive,
The gardens are in full bloom, as the flowers start to thrive;
And as we look around at the beauty that we see,
Remember spring brings Easter, when God's Son died on that tree.

Remember how He suffered, with those thorns upon His brow,
As the crowd kept shouting, 'Crucify Him,' it was an awful row;
How they made Him carry that cross to that hill outside the city,
Where they nailed His hands and feet to it, it was such a pity.

He hung there on that cross, the whole of that long day,
Though He was in pain, 'Father, forgive them,' was all He would say
He knew He had to die to forgive us all our sins,
So He hung up there in silence, knowing this battle He had to win.

Then came that glorious Easter day, when He rose from the dead,
He conquered death so we should know, death we shouldn't dread;
For just like Jesus on that Easter day, and the flowers in the spring,
We'll all rise again in glory, praise the Lord, let church bells ring.

Thelma Cook

I AM THE WAY

From cross to tomb
On the darkest day
And from tomb to glory
On a day of light
Christ showed the way.
The fear of death
No longer binds us
The freedom of the Son of God
Is ours, yours and mine
Now that we know the tomb
Is Heaven's womb
From which we are born
To a life divine.

Sean O'Kane

GOD'S GARDEN

The quiet churchyard is full of colour,
A sanctuary for birds, shrubs and spring flowers.
Wild flowers grow undisturbed in shady hollows,
Golden daffodils flourish amongst ancient gravestones
Moss, ferns, lichen and fungi
Dense on damp ground, growing naturally.
In tangled foliage birds build their nests
Lamb's-tails and hawthorn abundant on surrounding hedge.
Gusty march winds bend the tall trees
Which shelter the lovely old church, standing serene.
Spring sun glistens on stained glass windows
The open church door casting shadows.
Soon the Easter festival begins
Congregations will sing special Easter hymns.
Easter cards are sent, school holidays for children
Giving presents of Easter eggs an age old tradition
The colourful churchyard in full blossom
Surrounds the quiet church, standing in God's garden.

Lorna June Burdon

EASTER

My hero died upon a cross
He died to set us free
So we might live in His free world
And sing His praise
And feel His love
And as He died
A forgotten white flower
Lay upon the ground.

J M Stoles

EASTER TIME

Easter bunny is here again little children's eyes alight
To see bright packages their delight
As they rip the pretty wrappers to reveal
Delicious chocolate a tasty meal.

But Moms and Dads remind them too
Of the true meaning of Easter time
When Jesus died upon the cross
And rose again to save me and you.

Maggie Strong

THE JOY OF EASTER

Easter comes once a year
A time of love and peace is now here
Fun and play on Easter day
Singing in the church as well
So full of love you can tell
The sun shines down from the sky
This is love can't you see
The light of God for you and me
Spring brings in the lamb
Which lives in the farm
It is here in a manger
That Jesus was born
He was a great healer as you can see
He came here to save you and me
Now Easter is also a time of fun
Children roll their eggs down a hill
Then crack them open and eat their fill
I remember when I was young too
I painted pictures on my egg you see
And rolled it down the hill with glee
What a wonderful day for you and me.

Gordon Forbes

EASTER TIME

Easter is a lovely time,
With all the flowers around.
Cards and Easter eggs and cakes
Are always to be found.

But Easter is much more than this.
Good Friday Jesus died.
To save us all from sin
And give us hope within.

On the third day He rose again
To show there was a way.
For everyone to follow,
His commandments to obey.

The world is such a lovely place,
The stars, the moon, the skies.
The green fields and the mountains
Is what He has supplied.

So we should love one another,
Be to everyone a friend,
Do the good things He taught us,
Right to the very end.

Winifred Shore

THE SWING

Can you see the swing beneath the tree?
Can you see the sparrows fluttering free
And the white clouds scudding through the sky,
Or the grassy bank where the crocus lie?

Can you hear the sound of the taxi's horn,
Or the cry of a baby newly born?
See the swaying curls in a young girls hair?
Can you smell her perfume in the air?

Take a barefoot walk on morning grass.
Can you hear the bell for morning Mass
And see the folk wending their way
To the local church On Easter Day?

Will you count these blessing manifold,
Or wait until you're much too old
To give your thanks, or plan ahead?
Will you see the light when you are dead?

Did you ever wonder when in prayer
That maybe He might not be there.
Open your eyes if you want to see.
Can you see the swing beneath the tree?

Bernard Brady

EASTER

H unting for Easter eggs
A soft small chick
P alm Sunday
P ale eggs
Y ummy chocolate!

E njoy Easter eggs
A yellow fluffy newborn chick
S ome yummy Easter eggs
T asty soft Easter eggs
E aster top hat
R ose from the dead, Jesus.

Nathan Luetchford (8)

EASTER IS HERE

So spring is here
    it's the best time of the year
Still reminders of winter
    but promises of summer.

The sky seems bluer
    and the land is now greener
Bulbs are sprouting
    and the trees are budding.

Days are longer
    with more hours of light
The sun is stronger
    with shorter hours at night.

With Easter upon us
    the colours of flowers appear
Those dull dismal days of winter
    quickly disappear.

Soon spring turns to summer
    and our hope are raised
We feel so much better with nothing to fear
    spring at Easter *is* the best time of year.

Geoff Vineall

GOD LOVES US

Easter day a great day
A day Jesus resurrected
A day Jesus conquered death
A day Man got reunited to God
A day precious to man
A day that is unforgettable in our lives

On this day Satan's power was crushed
On this day Satan lost his pride
On this day God freed man from bondage
On this day salvation came unto Man
On this day peace was given unto Man
On this day things changed for Man

We owe God one thing
To emulate His love
To love others as He loved us
To live in peace as one
So that the world will be a better place
For His love He died for us

Ogbodo John Obinna

IT IS FINISHED

destroyed
ruined
wrecked
washed up

lost
broken
terminated
dead

over
ended
done
complete

fulfilled
concluded
accomplished
perfect

It is finished!

Mike Clifford

EASTER THOUGHTS

Hear the cry! Our Lord is risen! He's paid our debt on Calvary!
At first, we cannot understand our need for liberty!
For sin has been deceiving us! We think we're doing fine!
This life is our reality! What use is the Divine?
Who is this Jesus, anyway? What is it that He's done?
Do we believe the claims he's made? How could He be God's Son?
It's just a bit of fantasy! Let's push it all away,
For future consideration - not relevant today!

Jesus was an embarrassment. Does He embarrass you?
His Spirit reaches to our hearts - He knows all that we do!
Do you find that He's intrusive and won't leave you alone?
Are you longing for that freedom, to do things on your own?
When Jesus died upon that cross, darkness covered the Earth.
In a tomb they laid His body, awaiting its rebirth.
There's no way we can account for the Lord's Resurrection,
But it was clear, He placed Himself under God's direction!

God has a perfect, Sov'reign Will. His Spirit is divine.
He gave His Son to die for us - for your sake and for mine!
At Easter, we remember this - the sadness and the joy,
The sacrificial love of God, which nothing can deny.
He overcame the Devil's power, that we might be released
From every sin that holds us fast, bringing His perfect peace.
There's no greater name than Jesus, who takes away our sin.
He has an everlasting love! Will you not walk with Him?

Jenny Stevens

Easter Vigil

Something of the season's mystery -
Which offers up the consequence of resurrection
But keeps its secret: what happened in the tomb remains unspecified -
Meets me in the vigil that we keep on
Holy Saturday at Rowberrow:
A small church high in the hills, remote and
Set apart from houses, without streetlights, so
Stars are visible through and over leafless trees.
Inside perhaps two candles lit - enough to see which pew is free -
But otherwise a shadowed cave, silent except the chink of censer
being swung:
Scented by incense and by flowers, primroses covering the cover
of the font,
The rest pale glimmerings on the edge of sight.
We carry unlit candles out into the night, stumble over the
uneven graveyard,
Gather round the fire; flames stream sideways, hands cup and
shelter them.
'The light of Christ' 'Thanks be to God!'
We process, a flow of flickering, back into the church
And 'Christ is risen!'
It seems to me we touch the hem of Easter's robe, touch holiness,
As something great and grave that filled the sky to overflowing
Tabernacles with us underneath the rafters.

Susan Latimer

EASTER TIME

Following the forty days of penance
Having tried to do our best
The season of spring is here
So soon the calendar is set
But nature does not rest.

Easter a time of promise and rebirth
Our spirits soar to share the day
Will death's Grim Reaper come to stay
When once so promised and fulfilled
When the lamb of God was slain
Rejoice. Rejoice our Saviour's now with us
And so, will stay.

Children enjoying the festive season
With eggs and holidays
And watch the newborn lambs with wisdom
New life their innocence portrays
A symbol of our shepherd a sacrifice renewed.

E Saynor

LIFE'S TRIUMPH
(Thoughts On Easter)

God's life is potent in each living thing.
The humble plants safe wrapped in Earth's dark womb,
Responding to the light of Easter's spring
Burst forth as if all rising from the tomb.

The Saviour turns His steps towards the Cross
Along the road ordained for Him to tread,
Not heeding darts of malice men may toss
At Him who would their starving souls have fed.

Be still! Now comes the last dread sacrifice,
While ranks of watching angels hold their breath.

'Tis done. That life has paid the utmost price
For man's redemption from sin's power of death.

With love and joy before Thee Lord we lay
Our hearts, with Thee, new raised this Easter Day.

V E Godfrey

A Beloved Child

God's only begotten Son,
Brought Mary and Joseph great joy,
A child to lavish love upon,
A very precious boy.

He grew up with friends and foes,
And was led, with a cross - by a donkey,
To be hung on the Cross with a crown of thorns,
To suffer for the world to be free.

God resurrected His Son,
His body and soul are now above,
Whatever evil in the world is done,
He is always there, for us - with love.

D Carne

A Thought Of Spring

A snowdrop poking through the ground,
Through the hoar-frost all around.
And then I thought of spring.
The watery sun shone in the sky.
A lark was singing way up high
And then I thought of spring.
Gone were all those winter blues,
Gone all the 'bad weather' news.
Perhaps it's time to plan a cruise.
Now, that would be the thing.

How lovely it would be to say, 'Tomorrow we are on holiday',
Pack our bags, we're on our way.
Our 'plane is on the wing'.
We're sitting on some foreign shore, a book to read and drinks galore.
Who in the world could ask for more
From just 'a thought of spring'.

Joan Taylor

JOHN 19:19

I looked up,
there He was
watching me,
watching Him.
Jesus of Nazareth, the King of the Jews
Innocent blood was shed upon the cross.
Yes, crucified for expressing His views -
and the world will forever mourn His loss.
Splintered wood,
forsaken.
Save yourself!
Save us all!
Come down now
Son of God!
Take Him down -
torn in two.
Open arms,
He welcomed.
I looked up,
there He was.
His head bowed -
dying rose.
I looked down -
at His feet.

Olliver Charles

MESSIAH

He was a man of quiet dignity,
But possessed a powerful faith,
It's comforting to remember Him,
The massive sacrifices He made.

His worldly life was a short one,
But His love will reign forever,
At Easter time we think of Him,
The beloved Son of Man.

A lonely woman sat quietly,
Before a stony crop,
The doorway now rolled open,
A symbol of Christ's Heavenly love.

Catherine E Atkinson

THE THIRD DAY (II)

I was drowsy with dreams of angel's wings
then I heard a voice,
'Women, do not forsake your inheritance.
Wake up! Wake up! Wake up!'

(Weep and sleep)

We awoke from the stone-cold clasp of sleep
our eyes still weeping wetness,
wetness upon our soft skin
like the dew upon the leaves of Cyprus and olive groves.

Anger and fatigue wracked our souls,
resolute adjectives we could not shake
for fear that fear should consume us in its
hungry feast.

(Clay and flesh)

The dust clung to our feet as
we hurried on hard ground,
spices sweet and fragrant sifting
through our fingers, anointing the dust.

Then we saw it in the cold, cold
lightness of light - a stone!
We took a sharp intake of breath that
pierced our lungs and choked our tears.

(Stone and flesh)

The weight of our burdens rolled away,
fresh light swallowed
death's rank darkness
He was gone.

Our frames fell, collapsed, like shattered vessels
timid eyes dazzled by sweeps of brilliance,
then I saw the angel of my dreams
eternity's stillness released weeps of joy-laden tears.

(Salt and earth)

The stones are crying out!
Our hears of flesh, rendered, felt the glorious moment
He had risen just as He said.
He is alive! He is alive! He is alive!

Helen Thorn

EASTER INSPIRATIONS

Today I walked in a woodland glade,
Beneath the tall trees' leafy shade.
I wandered there disconsolate,
Pondering my cheerless fate.
My heart was sad, wondering when
Fortune would smile on me again.
A bird was singing high above,
Trilling out his song of love.
My eyes downcast upon the ground
Missed the beauty all around.
A scurrying rabbit startled me,
Lifting my eyes I then could see
The glory of a beech tree,
Spreading its branches over me.
A subtle perfume filled the air,
Primroses and violets fair
At my feet were growing there.
I stooped to pick the fragile flowers,
Then made my way home through the showers.
The sun came out and changed the scene,
My sad heart became serene.
This was God's creation, life re-born,
The wonder of a new spring morn.
I had eyes to see - beauty is free,
It is mine for the seeking!

Dora L Stuart

EASTER MEDITATION

Good Friday was
a wicked day
when God's own Son
our wages paid
for sins committed
by us all,
from birth to death
since Adam's fall.

But let us not
dwell in the past;
the pain and horror
did not last,
for three days later
Christ arose,
defiant, with
good proof to those
who scorned and mocked Him
when on earth,
the one who came
of noble birth,
to pay the price
for mankind's sins.

And now He knocks
to enter in
and share our lives
for evermore,
if we will open
our heart's door.

Allelujah!

Diana Lynch

THE MEANING OF EASTER

Jesus, I didn't realise
How much I was to blame
In crucifying You.
Sin required Your sacrifice
But my sin is the same,
Seen in the timelessness of God's
Eternal view.

And so, although I wasn't born
That dreadful day You died,
Each drop of blood You spilt,
Cruel nails and crown of thorn,
The spear thrust in Your side,
Seen in the timelessness of God
Were for my guilt.

Jesus, now that I understand
How much I was involved
My soul is horrified.
Although Your death was planned
How can I be absolved?
For in the timelessness of God
Where can I hide?

Jesus, since You have died for me,
Then I to self must die,
For You alone to live.
The Father's loving grace I see
Willing my debt to satisfy.
For in the timelessness of God
He can forgive.

John Goodspeed

THE HEAVENS WEPT

The heavens wept on Golgotha
The day Lord Jesus died,
And Peter heard again His words,
Three times He was denied.

The temple curtain rent in two
And the sky grew dark and black.
Thunder rolled around the Earth,
But He promised He'd be back.

In the Garden Of Gethsemane
They placed Him in a tomb,
But He rose on Easter Morning,
Glorious fruit of Mary's womb.

And He shall live for evermore,
Through every coming age.
We can write our own small part
On Heaven's Holy page.

Patricia Adele Draper

Easter Reflections

We come to church to meditate
And remember Jesus' plight
He who is the Son of God
Our Saviour, giving light.

The disciples who followed Him
Were sleeping, so did not see
When Jesus prayed to God above,
'Let this cup pass from me.'

'Crucify Him, crucify Him,'
Shouted people all around
But Pilate's proclamation was,
'In Him no fault is found.'

Yet, Jesus died upon the cross
In the place called Calvary,
The Good Shepherd who led His flock
And said, 'Just follow me.'

He died that we might be forgiven
For the sins of mortal life,
His selfless love is free for all
It takes away our strife.

The sadness of Good Friday
Jesus has risen above,
Easter Day is for rejoicing
As Christ feeds us with His love.

Peggy Courteen

Easter

The greatest festival of the year
What we did to the Son, we should all shed a tear
But renewal of life is thee celebration
Nature's blossom of green shoots throughout all the nation.

The bird keeps it warm, it's pride their to nestle
The symbol of life; a fertility vessel.
Roast cocoa bean from Mexican soil
Sweet oval egg wrapped in coloured tin foil.

Bright pretty cardboard packing up air
Concealing a meanness, spacial aware.
What is the true meaning, we all could discuss
While the great final feast would pass over us.

We now show our children this rather strange habit
These packaged surprises from mystical rabbit
Bring sticky fingers and sticky faces
Happy the children with their chocolate traces.

Ian Tiso

Easter 2000

Beside the lanes near Stowlangtoft
Cowslips grow profusion now
A splash of yellow in the green
Of verges verdant after rain.

Tree and shrubs are bursting out
Lark ascending - cloudscapes grand
Celebrate St George's Day
Triumph o'er the dragon slain.

And so to Boxford with the eggs
The Easter Bunny - magic spell
For tiny tot who's barely three
Grown ups too enjoyed the fun.

A family meal and then return
To Hadleigh on the twisting roads
Past Semer, Hincham, Bildeston
These names invoke a rural scene.

Steve Glason

PIETA

'See if there be any sorrow like unto my sorrow . . .'

She stood beneath the cross with Magdalene the sinner.
Immaculate, she could not weep.
Her heart pierced by a sword which
Weeping could not dull.

With hollow emptiness she watched,
Numb, but sentient, as her son was pierced
By the crown, the nails and the spear,
Each blow twisting the sword within her.

All was done. They gave Him limp
Into her arms. The life, the love,
Now a helpless, crooked corpse.
Six feet in height, He hung against her breast.
The light of the world was dimmed.
Who could relieve the darkness of her misery?

'See if there be any sorrow like unto my sorrow . . .'

Jane England

EASTER REMEMBERED

Christmas Day is three weeks past
and we are free of that at last,
but in the shops - a nasty shock -
they're filling up with lots of stock
of chocolate eggs and rabbits too.
Please tell me, what am I to do
to free myself from overkill
that's just designed to fill the till?
And this, at the expense of one
who some still know as God's own Son,
who, long ago, was crucified -
that's right, He really, truly died
upon a cross, outside the wall,
obedient to His Father's call.
So now I stand, bemused and numb,
to think that God Himself would come
to save the sinners and the dregs -
and all we think about is eggs!
The sinners still have need of Him,
although the memory's growing dim.
So stand with me this Eastertide -
remember God, who really died
and from his tomb, outside the wall,
came forth again to save us all.

Tim Nice

JUDAS

In dreams they stalk my dank and hollow veins:
the thin day's vapours cloaked in solid form.
Stooping, bowed hoods bent like poised scythes
they sniff the tell-tale trail of silver spoor.
Then mid the clicked denials of scuttling claws
they fall, muffled folds billowing, on brittle
thoughts that dragged like sins before the brink
of Ultimate Judgement, repent, gibber betrayal
then trace the caverns of this heart. I wake;

their misted breath behind my half-closed lids
like envoys from some deep stagnant mire
that ushered past the gaze of drowsing sentries,
nestle in the rushes of desire
licking the bloodless lintel of my brow,
enfolding blackened lips to consummate
a traitor's vow; seduced with silver coils
that deck the rim of dream-encumbered night,
sipping the starless waters of men's souls.

Chris Sherlock

SUNLIT GARDEN

On the Third Day
with perfumed shroud and
bitter tears she came,
To wash His feet and dry them
with her hair again . . .
But in that garden where
death had no place,
with sunlight warm
upon her face,
He came to her
and called her name . . .
And twice emancipated by
His grace,
rejoicing she became
first witness of
His Resurrection
In a garden
in the sun
On the Third Day.

Jo Lee

EASTER

God has chosen His garden of beauty, Easter to begin.
Carpets of golden daffodils on grass verges grow,
Bluebells and primroses their coloured dresses show.
Warm is the sun which shines down on the Earth,
Pale blue skies and pure white clouds.
Birds in their nests hatch out their eggs,
Grass is turning from brown to green
And flowers in the gardens grow,
While spring lambs frolic in the fields.
Birds in the trees and hedges sing,
'Wake up it's Easter and it's spring.'
God show His love for us in all things,
No wonder the mother bird sings.

Doreen Petherick Cox

Easter Promise

Far away beyond the night
A city descends with golden light.
To this dark world of weary men
God sends a new Jerusalem.

With crystal waters and streets of gold,
Unsurpassed beauty to behold.
A city not in need of sun,
Nor stars and moon when day is done.

The sands of time are running fast,
All will be new, the old has passed.
Jesus Christ the Living Word
Shall rule the world with two-edged sword.

Forgotten shall the dark age be
When they led Our Lord to Calvary.
It was there He died and paid for sin
So new life for us will now begin.

All creation then will be as new
The perfect flower with morning dew.
Creatures frolic on forest floor
Birds will sing as never before.

This is the message that Easter brings
With dove of peace on snow-white wings.

Greta Gaskin

PALMS OF JERICHO

Perhaps they brought from Jericho
The palms they threw beneath the hooves.
Perhaps they waved them up the road
The pilgrims bound for Zion.

Perhaps they watched Him lead the way
Disciples full of fear and awe,
'Let us go and die with Him
And cast our cloaks before Him.'

Perhaps we, too, should trophies bring
And leave behind the city of palms
To reach the gates, 'Hosanna' cry -
And follow as the echoes die.

Christopher Payne

THE JOY OF EASTER

Easter time is special, it brings us lots of joy,
It warms the hearts of people, each parent, girl and boy.
It holds a mystic wonder, such pleasures can be found,
The air is warm and even and happiness around.
The church is filled with wonder as people go to pray,
At Easter time, a special time, a very special day.
To thank the Lord for Easter and joy that it will bring,
To gaze in wonder at the cross, to hear the choirs sing.
Easter time is special, and spring is in the air,
People praise the risen Lord with gratitude and care.
Shops are filled with presents, with Easter eggs and cards,
Everyone is happy, and nothing can be marred.
The sacrifice by Jesus Christ that we may live gain
He suffered long upon the cross, his body wrecked with pain.
The resurrection of the Lord has helped us to believe,
His life on Earth was not in vain, we should not sit and grieve.

We visit old aged people and take them gifts of love,
It brings us joy and happiness, with blessings from above.
Forgetting not the hospitals, the homeless who can't cope,
We make their lives so thankful and fill them all with hope.
Easter time is special, the turkey and the wine,
The Easter decorations bring out this special time.
If every day was Easter and people filled with glee,
The world would be contented, a happy place to be.
Easter time is special, it brings us peace and love,
The Lord indeed has risen, with blessings from above.

Marjorie Picton

SAD

I'm so sad I go for a walk, the sun tells me to cheer up and gives me a wave,
The grass says, 'Stop crying, things can't be that bad.'

I give a half-hearted smile and walk on.

A tulip stops to ask my name, 'None of your business,' I say.
A tiny bird lands on my shoulder and kisses my cheek, she then flies off to her friends.

Why is everyone and everything so happy when I'm sad?

What's that? A daisy whispering, 'I love you,' to another daisy.
I see a ladybird, she looks so bright and beautiful. 'Come on,' she says, 'It can't be that bad.'
She flies off towards the sun.
A sunflower bends towards me to tell me to watch the children on the swings.

I watch and laugh, I feel so happy, it's Easter, everything and everyone is happy and so am I.
Was I sad? I can't remember.

Cassy Bailey

NEW LIFE

Life's road is bumpy, full of bends
Our destination all depends
On negotiating this hazardous track
With a straight and strengthened back
Don't be bowed and don't be sad
Lift your head - be glad, be glad
Ladybirds and butterflies
Bring joy and colour to our eyes
Young green leaves upon the trees
Gentle humming of the bees
Plants are bursting into life
Resurrection through the strife
I have life and I have love
I have peace from above

Maryska Carson

JESUS: A PRAYER TO HIMSELF

Stones of suffering cut my feet
Sea of despair damped my hair
Sand of sorrow blinded my vision
Sun of rejection burned my back
Wind of pain hit my face
Frost of loneliness bit my skin
Rain of misery soaked my soul.

Shone down by the moon of blame
Belted by hailstones of hate
Whispering grass of slander murmured my name
Fell in the puddle of desolation
Climbed the trees of sadness
Slept in the branches of failure.

Walked the Earth and lasted the seasons,
I have not crumbled to the bearers of false tidings
Nor bowed my head to the man holding the sword of emotion
My spirit is my light
My soul is my hope
My heart is my life.

Matteo Sedazzari

Easter

In the breeze of spring you are there
In the whisper of my garden, in the cool evening air.

When daffodils bloom as bright as the sun
My thoughts turn to the Holy chosen one.

A man with such love so pure and rare
Sacrificed for us mere mortals
His world left bare.

Crucified for us, sinners
We realised and we wept
Redeem us oh Lord
In your heart we are kept.

We are restored through your rising
Our souls are set free
May God reign supreme
For all eternity.

Bernadette Woehrle

AN EASTER RECIPE

Just another April morning:
Sweet phrases of birdsong
Pierce the deathly moments of silence;
Soft streaks of sunlight
Merge with insinuating shadows;
Golden daffodils dance on the hilltop,
Ash-white lilies line the valleys;
New birds, new blossoms, new life
Fighting the ghosts of winter's carnage.

Just another April morning:
A field of fragile lambs
Watched by the wary mother ewes;
A green hillside of dewy grass
Cradling three skeletal trees;
A musical stream of silvery water
Running red with the blood of a dead lamb;
Such sorrow, such pain,
Such joy and everlasting hope.

Sarah Dodds

Chicken Or The Egg

A delicate example of life's creations,
The birth of a fragile chick,
Into a world of new sensations,
Of which it cannot pick,
It doesn't know how it will be used,
The dinner table or to keep the kids amused,
No wonder it's bemused,
Wishing to retreat back into its shell
From which its birth was fused.

But new life is how people learn,
A young child is not to know,
Experience is something you earn,
Paying for decisions as you grow,
Some may say the meaning of Easter is lost
As spring sunshine replaces winter frost,
It cannot surely be a commercial toy,
As I share my young goddaughter's joy,
Chocolate eggs are just unhealthy for me,
But she can tuck in with such innocent glee!

Neil West

EASTER TIME

The cold, dark days of winter have gone,
It's sunny forever
Or am I wrong?

The weather won't change
Whatever we say,
All that I know
Is that it's Easter day.

Everyone's happy
Filling their tummies,
With chocolate eggs
And Easter bunnies.

I hope you enjoy
This special day,
With you and your family
That's all I can say.

Ben Wilkinson (9)

INRI (JESUS NASARENUS REX JUDAEORUM)

If I could tell you about
A Christ who is a knight
Standing on his mount
His sceptre in his hand
And a decimated army under his feet

If I could tell you about
A Christ who is a boxer
His fist closed
Braving all his opponents

If I could tell you about
A Christ who is a superhero
Gliding on the air
And running to save people in danger

If I could tell you about
A Christ who is a superstar
Making daydreams in his thousands of fans

If Jesus Christ was only one of these persons
I would have nothing to tell you today
But I talk about the son of God
A King who is ready to meet

Ntamack Serge

FROM OBSCURITY INTO THE LIGHT

Stop and listen to the tempo of nature,
As it weaves its melody around us,
Feel its vibrations,
As it dances with exquisite joy,
No longer restrained by its captor,
Freedom is its song.

Growth, like the phoenix,
Rises from the barren wasteland,
Energy emanates,
Transmits the signal,
Produced by the artist nature,
Ripples of harmony abound.

Valiantly the captive
Struggles forth
From its gloomy cell,
Where incarcerated for a time,
Life born of a season's death,
Imprisoned by the winter reaper.

Spring signals rebirth
Into yet another stage,
Life is but a circle,
A regeneration of that once terminated,
Just as life and death
Are but a continuation.

We too will experience
Earthly death,
And, in faith, will enter the light and beyond,
To live once more and rejoice,
In the blessings of that Good Friday long ago,
Our Lord Jesus made this possible.

Ann G Wallace

ROYAL COLOURS

White and gold for Eastertide, to crown the waking Earth.
White snowdrops, 'February Maids' the warming soil gives birth.
Gold crocuses and daffodils with March's gales will bear,
In valleys and on icy downs spring's message they declare.
Though pain and sorrow still may come,
Though muted be our praise -
'My God, why hast Thou forsaken me?'
Thy hands my soul shall raise.

Kathleen M Hatton

Blooming World

The blooming world all gone wrong
Lord look upon
time for frolics
time for cheers
blooming flowers everywhere
an egg at Easter
the Lord's Prayer,
time for lambs, the farmer cheers,
our work is never done
filling the nation's tums.

J Evans

EASTER CHRISTENING
(Dedicated to Lucy Amber)

Sleep in peace - little one
whilst the world worries around you.
Dream gently - little one
love's blanket wrapped around you.

Wake smiling - little one
fill your world with laughter.
Take care - little one
guard that happiness hereafter.

Leigh Crighton

THE CROWNED PRINCE OF EARTH

He crowned unbidden, 'The King of Kings',
Not with one of gold and precious stones,
But one made from vicious thorns
Which saw his blood flow like tears.
A scene surreal; from forehead to eyes,
His head, in pain and humiliation bowed.
Pilate asking the milling, jeering crowds,
'Which condemned man must we save?'
Conspirators sent from the priesthood
Began to shout, 'Barabbas, Barabbas!'
Jesus condemned to die on the cross.
Mankind at that moment given salvation,
At the time of our greatest loss.
This already written in the Good Book,
By Heaven and the ever vigilant stars.
Jesus, in His preaching, had always said
His true realm was never here
Within this Earthly kingdom,
Rather here on a limited stay,
A prince on an informal visit,
First in the guise of a poor carpenter,
Becoming the wise and benign teacher,
A miracle worker healing the sick,
A kindly shepherd tending his flock,
A brief visit, to an untimely death,
His wise words, a string of pearls,
Evermore encircling the fecund Earth.
A rosary, handed down the fleeing centuries,
Easter morning, golden glory, bells pealing out,
Such joyful news, He has risen from the tomb.

Julia Pegg

EASTER AND SPRINGTIME

I love . . .

March winds and April showers heralding
the freshness of Easter blowing in on invigorating air,
painting a new spring green,
tender and serene
and the soft, delicate blossoms welcomed by the trees,
splashing colours, pink and white,
on the outgoing bleakness as
new life pushes forth with eager delight,
joyous to have arrived,
through the chain of creation.

I hate . . .

The chocolate eggs in familiar, boring boxes,
undeniably the same print run from the previous year,
containing chocolate bars bearing no connection to the
Easter feeling and
hot cross buns with a careless, topsy-turvy cross,
having been on sale since January 1st with
the fluffy, frivolous, money-spinning toys, chicks and ducks,
latching on for the making of quick bucks.

I love . . .

My sweet saviour, Jesus,
My teacher, my guide,
And the story of His donkey ride.

Carol Ann Darling

Chocoholic

I confess I'm just a hopeless chocoholic,
Put some Dairy Milk before me and it's gone,
It's the stuff that ruins waistlines without number,
So bang goes another diet I was on.

Inside each tasty packet of Maltesers
Is a little voice which says, 'Eat all of me.'
Give me the slightest glance at any double Mars bar,
That's the place you've got to look if you've lost me.

Take Magnum Seven Deadly Sins type ice cream,
Plus a Twix bar and a chocolate nougat too,
Mix them well and add them to my lunchtime sandwich,
If you're lucky, I might save a bite for you.

I have thought about a cure for all my sinning,
And less chocolate means more money I've not spent,
So for now to prove that I can really do it,
I have given chocolate eating up for Lent!

__Gillian Humphries__

LOVE BEYOND OUR MEASURE

How big is love? How deep? How wide?
How high? How strong? Can we decide?
How smooth? How rough? How loud? How still?
Working with, or against our will?

How big is love? How deep? How wide?
How much? How little to heal the divide?
Where does love start? Where does love end?
Is love our enemy? Is love our friend?

How big is love? How deep? How wide?
Is love to keep or share outside
These four walls? That's my choice,
To hear your answers, hear your voice.

How big is love? How deep? How wide?
That the Creator of all was He who died
To open the doors and chest of treasure;
Love beyond our knowledge, love beyond our measure.

Stuart Wood

REAWAKENING

Like Lancaster bombers
off on a mission,
swans take off

along the runway
of the canal
with a great

flapping of wings,
long necks outstretched
towards the sun.

Some snow lingers.
Beneath the hedge,
blackbirds scratch about,

searching for earthworms,
creating a hubbub
of dead leaves.

The strengthening sun
will make excavation
easier for them.

Some seven-spot ladybirds
emerge from hibernation,
the milder weather

setting them off
on a leaf-crawl.
It's still too cold, however,

for flying lessons
of for snapping open
their tiny wings.

Norman Bissett

FOR ME

And Hell was black
and the Father turned his back
and it was shameful
and You looked pitiful
Lord You hung there
You hung there

You could have split Heaven
You didn't have to be there
and people mocked
at what they did not understand
Lord You hung there
just for me

The day was black
and the Earth quaked
Bitter wine they gave You
and the lashes on Your back hurt so
Lord You hung there
just for me

In shame You went down
with glory You came up
Lord You overcame
for me

Adedotun Adejuyigbe

Jesus Is Lord

God's Son has risen - a beautiful day begins
And the grace of God is full of eternal love
The Messiah I speak of is Jesus Christ the *Lord*
He is the Son of God and Saviour of all mankind
Messiah has risen from the dead and has washed and cleansed
My soul, my life, my all to King Jesus
    Praise the *Lord*.

He has promised His living Word for mankind
The place in Messiah will be my home
So I will follow King Jesus
Wherever His will
I am trusting in the *Lord* Jesus
To meet my every need
Christ has risen
The last day is very near
King Jesus is coming soon
The gates of Heaven will burst open
King Jesus will lead us home
To welcome His children
    Praise to God

For He has given us life on the Mount of Olives
There He paid the price for you and me
For all sinners His blood was shed on the tree
To give us eternal life
Our Saviour and *Lord* and King
Christ has died
Christ has risen
Christ will come again for those who wait for Him
    Praise the *Lord*

Deirdre Banda

IN PRAISE OF EASTER

Green grass growing,
Soft breeze blowing,
Jesus is alive!

Tall trees swaying
Children playing,
Jesus is alive!

Young dogs prancing,
Flower heads dancing,
Jesus is alive!

Birds' song lifting,
White clouds drifting,
Jesus is alive!

Bombs exploding,
Guns reloading,
Jesus is alive!

Millions hungry,
Death to Sunday,
Jesus is alive!

Young wife grieving,
Addicts pleading,
Jesus is alive!

Love descending,
Man rejecting,
Jesus is alive!

Love arising,
Man accepting,
Jesus *is* alive!

Sandra J Walker

THE FORGOTTEN EASTER

Easter eggs on Sunday,
Any kind will do.
Sweets covered in milk chocolate,
Treats for me and you
Enjoying the season's hot cross buns.

Religious reasons for the day,
    Zero, nothing, none.

Everyone forgets the day
A man died on the cross,
Saving the world from sin and pain,
Tragic though the loss,
Enjoying the eggs and hot cross buns.

Religious reasons for the day,
    Zero, nothing, none.

Kathleen Townsley

THE GLORY OF THE EASTER STORY

In the glorious Easter story
A troubled world can find
Blessed reassurance
And enduring peace of mind . . .
For though we grow discouraged
In this world we're living in,
There is comfort just in knowing
God has triumphed over sin . . .
For our Saviour's resurrection
Was God's way of telling men
That in Christ we are eternal
And in Him we live again.

And to know life is unending,
And God's love is endless too,
Makes our daily tasks and burdens
So much easier to do . . .
For the blessed Easter story
Of Christ the living Lord,
Makes our earthly sorrow nothing
When compared with this reward,
It's the promise of life eternal.

Rose Vincent

LAMENT IN RESURRECTION

You let them take me away
Put me on the cross of pain
Sentenced before I was even tried
Fate already known, gonna be crucified

All that's left is the statue in effigy
Of me sacrificed on the hill of Galilee
Just a simple man who died on a cross
Not a soldier of hate, a bringer of love

Then you tried to absolve the misery
Who was it that turned away?
Couldn't bear to look, hid their shame
And still you repent to this day

I died so you all could live in peace
Now all you can do is mock me
You didn't know or want to believe
Yet you celebrate my death each year

What was the point in my dying?
What was the point in all the crying?
I came to teach you all peace and love
But you still hate and the wars go on

Remember as the eggs roll down the hill
You can roll away hate if you have the will
What has it come to symbolize and realise
Then eternal peace and love will be your prize

David McDonald

An Easter Dawn

Whispers upon a spring breeze
Voice of an Easter dawn
Danced upon the willow's leaves
As He was reborn.

Pleasantly Saviour woken
Under clear heavenly sky
All listen God has spoken
Such words tears to the eye

As darkness does risk a peek
Rejoice the Son returned
Chattering language of the meek
The world a lesson learned

For Judas a surprise
In exchange for pieces of thirty
Not death but a reprieve
Still forgiveness of hands dirty

Always the inspiration
That good will win
Forever the celebration
The end of sin

He who shared His vision
At which we all gaze
Understanding His mission
Forever to embrace His ways

Paul McLynn

EASTER IS HERE!

'Easter is here!' says the garish sign
If it was just a custom that would be fine
But it's all about a corporation getting your cash
For the New Year's/Christmas/Easter stash.

'Easter is here!' It's January you fool
Like early summer, 'Welcome back to school'
And even now a girl with tree trunk legs
Is stuffing her fat face with Cadbury's Creme Eggs.

'A little Easter chick, Mummy!' 'No, we need to hurry.'
Today's Easter chick is tomorrow's chicken curry.
That kid's room is awash with toys of yesterday
Tacky themed rubbish bought in seasonal fray

10 per cent Easter egg, 90 per cent box
Its producers have just died from smallpox
Nestlé took the main cut, the family's bereavement
Was losing their land to a 'Free Trade Agreement'.

So the Easter holiday finally starts for me
And tacky holiday programming starts on TV
We seem to get these holidays but don't know why
And will you please tell what this has to do with this funny Jesus guy?

Duncan Catterall

EASTER MUSIC
(From a country organist)

Easter brings forth gold and airy blossoms
small petals lying in the breeze
I hear
the mewl of a lamb, the bleat of a ewe,
the liquid pearls of the blackbird,
hidden water tinkling on pebbles leading me to the tiny church
protected by the splendid manor
I hear
a low creak as the porch door opens
lily scented darkness
and flickering candles
I hear
the organ sounds with low drawn chords under
sweet ephemeral notes
floating upwards
trapping a lazy butterfly in lengthy bars of smoky dust drops
I hear
the Easter people, bright hats bobbing, whispered greetings
(priest resplendent in satiny white)
voices blending, filling the nave with harmony
'Jesus Christ is risen today' swells forth with lusty vigour
telling the crucifixion story with its cruel end
in three short verses
I hear
'Alleluia' and the final glorious notes
dispelling gloom and forty days of suffering,
taking us forward to the hopefulness of spring.

Clare Dawson

EASTER RESOLUTION

Easter holidays were fast approaching,
I wanted a break from my dull, boring life,
I sat on the beach away from the crowd,
Wanting to plan a lovely holiday.
A visit to Hawaii, yachting in the Caribbean,
The Grand Canyon, and pyramids of Egypt,
Passed through my mind for me to choose.
The waves so high, frothing at my feet,
Emerged from the ocean emerald green,
The sky was bright with stars and moon,
Pulled an unknown string in my heart,
What is happiness that really counts?
Is it just chasing shortcut pleasures?
Driving happily without seeing the watch,
Through the freeway to wherever I want,
Or doing whatever money could provide?
I need something more for lasting happiness,
In vain I search that sacred joy,
In selfish pleasures packed with pain,
I closed my eyes in serene meditation,
My old mother stood there smiling,
Working silently running the orphanage,
Wiping the tears of the discarded children,
Is this the secret of her joy so radiant?
Is this the source of her immense energy?
Is service to needy service to God?
I made a resolution to visit the orphanage,
Buy gifts for the children and my mum,
The very thought of it filled me with joy,
That gives meaning to a meaningless life.

P K Janaky

AN EASTER PRAYER

You bore the pain with love alone,
Its purpose - love to prove,
Upon the tree in agony,
Yet still Man is not moved.

O gentle one in paradise,
Let Your love solve once more,
Revitalise the faith in Man,
To reach that Heaven's door.

What You with love have won for us,
So dearly on the cross,
Give us the strength Your love sustain,
To fight against its loss.

Mary Hughes

INFORMATION

We hope you have enjoyed reading this book - and that you will continue to enjoy it in the coming years.

If you like reading and writing poetry drop us a line, or give us a call, and we'll send you a free information pack.

Alternatively if you would like to order further copies of this book or any of our other titles, then please give us a call or log onto our website at www.forwardpress.co.uk

**Triumph House Information
Remus House
Coltsfoot Drive
Peterborough
PE2 9JX
(01733) 898102**